Music, Fashion, and Style

Matt Anniss

A+
Smart Apple Media

Published by Smart Apple Media, an imprint of
Black Rabbit Books
P.O. Box 3263, Mankato, Minnesota 56002
www.smartapplemedia.com

Published by arrangement with the Watts Publishing
Group LTD, London.

Library of Congress Cataloging-in-Publication Data
Anniss, Matt.
 Music, fashion, and style / by Matt Anniss.
    pages cm. – (The music scene)
 Includes index.
 Summary: "Describes how musicians and perform-
ers become fashion icons and sway trends among
teens. Explains how teens identify with a genre or
musical movement and dress the part. Case studies
follow the influence of Madonna, the Sex Pistols, and
Grace Jones"– Provided by publisher.
 ISBN 978-1-59920-912-8 (library binding)
1. Rock music–Social aspects–Juvenile literature.
2. Musicians–Clothing–History–20th century–Juvenile literature. 3. Teenagers–Clothing–History–20th
century–Juvenile literature. 4. Fashion–History–
20th century–Juvenile literature. I. Title.
 ML3534.A545 2015
 306.4'8424–dc23
                                    2013022575

ISBN 978-1-59920-912-8 (library binding)
ISBN 978-1-62588-591-3 (eBook)

Dewey Classification: 306.4'8424

Printed in the United States by CG Book Printers
North Mankato, Minnesota

PO 1720
PO 2-2015

9 8 7 6 5 4 3 2 1

Acknowledgments:
The publisher would like to thank the following
for permission to reproduce photographs:
Corbis: Condé Nast Archive 20bl, Henry Diltz
19bl, Sunset Boulevard 13tr; Dreamstime: Daniel
Garcia 6tr, ImageCollect 14tr, Sean Pavone 32bl,
Jose Antonio Sánchez Reyes 33tl, Aaron Settipane
37tr; Getty Images: Redferns 24tr; Istockphoto:
Izabela Habur 15br; Library of Congress: United
Press International 10; Rex Features: Rick Colls
28bl, Everett Collection 8bl, Fraser Gray 23tr,
Julian Makey 31bl, Ilpo Musto 12bl, Armando
Pietrangeli 9b, Suzy del Campo / PYMCA 31tr,
Sipa Press 16bl, Ray Stevenson 21tr, Richard Young
40tr; Shutterstock: Yuri Arcurs 23br, Chaoss 6bl,
ChinellatoPhoto 42br, Dfree 34br, Elisanth cover,
Featureflash 7br, 41cr, Adam Helweh 27br, iPhoto
Digital Events 5br, 38bl, Lemony 29tr, R. Gino Santa
Maria 26tr, Nejron Photo 35tr, Photobank.ch 22br,
Photoproject.eu 17cr, Lev Radin 33br, Joe Seer 19tr,
Gordana Sermek 18cr, Nikola Spasenoski 36tr;
Wikipedia: Jose Garcia 25br, H. Grobe 11cr, Fabio
Venni 30bl.

Every attempt has been made to clear copyright.
Should there be any inadvertent omission please
apply to the publisher for rectification.

CONTENTS

Chapter One: Fashion and Pop 6
Fashion Revolution.....................8
The British Influence 10
Glamour Boys and Girls....................12
TV Fashion 14
Industry Case Study: Madonna 16
Chapter Two: Peace, Love, and Hate....18
Industry Case Study: The Sex Pistols 20
Two Tribes................................22
Rough Trade 24
Chapter Three: Beat the Street..............26
This is Acid 28
Tuning In 30
Big in Japan................................32
Web Style 34
Chapter Four: Big Business....................36
Industry Case Study: Grace Jones......38
The Brit Scene 40
Industry Case Study: Lady Gaga 42
Glossary 44
Further Reading 45
Index...46

CHAPTER ONE

FASHION AND POP

On street corners, hip-hop fans hang out in their baggy jeans, sneakers, and baseball caps. Across town, a group of techno dance fans head to a rave in skinny jeans, colorful tops, and eclectic jewelry. Elsewhere, a group of skateboarders head to a punk concert.

The grunge-inspired style, originally made famous by Seattle bands in the early 1990s, continues to be popular decades later.

Dress to Impress

For music fans around the world, their clothing, hair, and makeup choices are often influenced by the sounds that come out of their iPod earphones. Many music fans believe following a band or a style of music is about belonging to a special group. Being a goth, punk, hip-hop, or heavy metal fan gives them a sense of **identity**. Just as sports fans wear the colors of their favorite team, music fans also want people to know about their passion.

Goth style is as popular with today's teenagers as it was 30 years ago.

Distinctive Clothing

But there has always been more to the relationship between music and fashion than simply wanting to be part of a group. The musicians who set the trends have no need to fit in with a crowd. They wear the clothes that make them feel good, or help them to make a statement.

Love the Style

Music, fashion, and style are forms of **creative expression**. It's no coincidence that all three are closely linked. After all, who hasn't watched a great music video and fallen in love with not just the song, but also with the clothes, the style of the band?

Get the Look

Top musicians want their own "look." To help them achieve this, they may work with leading fashion designers or stylists. The clothes they wear must be distinctive, but also appeal to would-be fans. If fans like what they see, they'll want to buy and wear the same clothes, or get the same haircut.

The Scoop

In March 2011, Britney Spears faced trouble following the launch of her fragrance, Radiance. A company called Brand Sense said that she'd broken a contract with them to make the perfume. They sued her for $10 million. Spears eventually paid an undisclosed amount to the company.

Big-Money Deals

Some music stars launch their own clothing labels. Hip-hop billionaires such as Jay-Z, 50 Cent, and P. Diddy have all supplemented their income from music by launching their own fashion companies.

Coming Up

In this book, we'll reveal how certain famous looks came about, how pop stars constantly change the way we all dress, and why clothing stores look to music scenes for inspiration. We'll also explain how top musicians make millions of dollars through deals with clothing, perfume, and makeup companies.

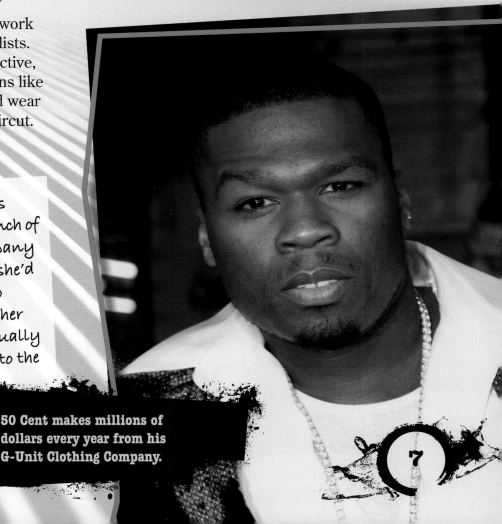

50 Cent makes millions of dollars every year from his G-Unit Clothing Company.

7

FASHION REVOLUTION

Music, fashion, and style have not always been linked. During the first half of the 20th century, there was little or no distinct **pop culture**. All of that changed in the 1950s, thanks to a revolutionary form of music called rock and roll.

Not for Parents

Musically, rock and roll didn't appeal to the older generation. Teenagers and young people liked it because it was loud, fun, and great to dance to. And because their parents disliked the music, more and more young people started getting into rock and roll.

Role Models

Rock and roll is important because it was about more than just music. Many rock and roll stars had their own distinct style that was soon copied by young people. Singers such as Gene Vincent and Elvis Presley wore tight jeans, white T-shirts, and leather jackets. They slicked their hair back or sculpted it into quiffs using hair gel and wax, such as Brylcreem.

Movie Magic

The influence of rock and roll went further than the songs of Elvis or Buddy Holly. The look and attitude of rock-and-roll-loving teenagers quickly became a big part of popular Hollywood movies, too. Films such as *Rock Around the Clock*, *Jailhouse Rock* (starring Elvis Presley), *Don't Knock the Rock*, and *Blue Denim* all featured teenage heroes who lived for music and fashion.

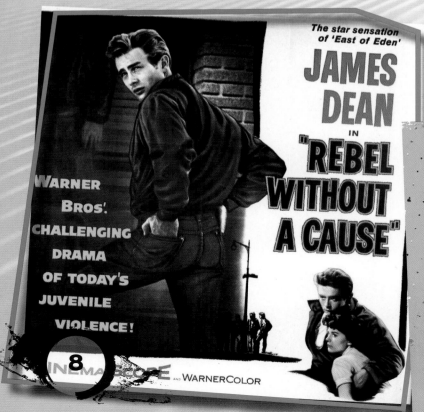

The star sensation of 'East of Eden'
JAMES DEAN
IN
"REBEL WITHOUT A CAUSE"
WARNER BROS'. CHALLENGING DRAMA OF TODAY'S JUVENILE VIOLENCE!
CINEMASCOPE AND WARNERCOLOR

Rebel Role Model

Perhaps the most *influential* movie of the era was 1955's *Rebel Without a Cause*, starring James Dean. In the film, he played a teenager who argued with his parents, dressed like a rock star, and stood up to local bullies. The film was a runaway success. It made popular the idea of the rebel teenager who lived for rock and roll and dressed to impress.

Teddy Boys

In the UK, rock-and-roll-obsessed teens were called Teddy Boys. They dressed differently than US rockers. They liked to wear long drape jackets with velvet trim, **drainpipe trousers**, white shirts, narrow ties, and low-heeled shoes, such as brogues.

British Teddy Boys had a lot in common with US rock and roll fans, spending just as much time on their clothes and hair. Yet Teddy Boys took the rock and roll attitude to the extreme. They hung out in gangs and sometimes caused trouble, fighting among themselves or with authority figures.

Teenage Kicks

The fashion and style that formed around rock and roll music was a starting point for future teen music and fashion trends. Ever since the 1950s, fans of both popular and less well-known musical styles have tried to stand out by dressing differently. Today's teenage music fans, whether they are into hip-hop, goth, or rave, owe a lot to the **pioneers** of rock and roll.

In the late 1950s, British Teddy Boys defined themselves by the clothes they wore and the rock and roll music they listened to.

9

THE BRITISH INFLUENCE

If the rock and roll revolution of the 1950s launched the concept of the teenager, the 1960s cemented the relationship between young people, music, and fashion.

High Life

Many UK music fans couldn't afford the latest London fashions, but they could afford the clothes sold in department stores. These clothes were inspired by the latest pop trends, such as miniskirts and **double-breasted** suit jackets. Young fashion became a booming business worldwide, as more and more teenagers tried to look like their idols.

Surf's Up

In the early 1960s, pop fashion moved away from the aggressive look of rockers, toward a more "clean-cut" look. This was largely due to the success of US bands such as The Beach Boys, whose songs about surfing and hot rods **promoted** a wholesome way of life. Their look of casual pants, jackets, and short-sleeved shirts reflected this ideal.

The British are Coming

The clean-living image of The Beach Boys was a major influence on a band that became worldwide leaders in pop fashion—The Beatles. They'd grown up in Liverpool, UK, as rockers in leather jackets, but their manager, Brian Epstein, wanted them to replace their rough-edged style with a more respectable look.

The Beatles' choice of clothes and "mop-top" haircuts changed the way many people around the world dressed.

10

Beatlemania

Because Epstein wanted The Beatles to look smart, he dressed them in collarless suits designed by the finest **tailors** in London. He added specially designed Beatle boots and mop-top haircuts. As The Beatles' fame spread, these trends became popular with young people all over the world.

Swinging London

The success of British bands in the United States helped to make London the most fashionable place on the planet. By the middle of the 1960s, **mainstream** fashions on both sides of the Atlantic were being set by the bands that shopped on the King's Road in Chelsea or Carnaby Street in Soho.

In the 1960s, the King's Road in Chelsea, London, boasted some of the most trendsetting clothing shops in the world.

Vintage Look

In recent years, the pop fashions of 1960s London have become popular again. This is due to the vintage **revival** seen in a number of modern pop stars. Perhaps the first to hit the headlines was singer Amy Winehouse, whose look and sound reached back to the glory days of 1960s pop.

The Scoop

One of the most famous "mod" bands of all time, The Who, wrote an album and film about the **rivalry** between old-fashioned rockers and mods who preferred the new **R&B** music. It was called Quadrophenia, and it told the story of one young mod's struggle against rockers and the **establishment** in the United Kingdom.

GLAMOUR BOYS AND GIRLS

Pop in the 1970s was a multi-colored mix of sing-along rock and glamorous, disco-inspired dance music. As it had in the 1950s and '60s, fashion followed music. This time, it wasn't just teenagers dressing to impress, but people of all ages.

Glam Jam

In the first half of the 1970s, so-called "glam rock" acts such as David Bowie, Iggy Pop, Alice Cooper, T. Rex, and Lou Reed caught headlines. David Bowie set the trend of wearing platform boots, jumpsuits, and glitter makeup.

Flare Up

It was the boldness of the clothes that really caught on. Flared bell-bottom pants, wide ties, and brightly colored shirts were the clothes of choice for men in Western Europe and the United States.

The Scoop

London-based designer Mary Quant shaped the way women dressed in the 1970s. She first became famous in the 1960s for inventing the miniskirt. She then found further fame by introducing the world to hot pants—tiny, tight shorts that became popular during the disco era.

With his love for outrageous clothes and eccentric makeup, singer David Bowie had a profound effect on the way men dressed in the 1970s.

Hot Things

Women wore equally glamorous outfits, often featuring flared satin pants, leather miniskirts, and glittery blouses or crop tops. In keeping with the musical fashion of sparkle and eyeliner, women also wore super-bright makeup.

Tartan Army

In the mid-1970s, one particular pop group set an unlikely trend of wearing tartan, a traditional Scottish fabric used for making **kilts**. The Bay City Rollers were a teen pop group from Edinburgh, Scotland, whose fame spread to the United States in 1976. As a sign of support, many of their teenage female fans would wear tartan scarves, traditional Scottish hats, and even tight tartan pants!

Disco Fever

As the 1970s progressed, the pop charts became dominated by disco. This was a form of US dance music that began in New York City. Disco stars had their own unique dress sense, with men wearing a new version of the classic three-piece suit. To make the style more contemporary, designers added wide collars to shirts and flared bottoms to pants.

Man-made Style

Throughout the 1970s, music stars influenced the popularity of clothes made from man-made fabrics such as **polyester**, nylon, and Lycra. These clingy, often tight-fitting fabrics were revolutionary because they could be used to make fashions that had never been seen before.

Saturday Night Dance

The classic disco look was made popular by the film *Saturday Night Fever*, which featured John Travolta as a neighborhood disco-dancing champion. Travolta's famous outfit became the **blueprint** for men's clothing the world over. Soon, everyone was wearing three-piece suits, tight flared trousers, and brightly colored polyester shirts.

13

TV FASHION

In the 1980s, the relationship between pop and fashion heated up. Music Television, known as MTV, created an even bigger explosion for many fashion trends. Music videos pushed the costumes and styles of music stars into millions of living rooms around the world, influencing people everywhere.

Michael Jackson's music videos were hugely popular in the 1980s, leading many teenagers to copy his dance moves and bold choice of clothing.

Music Makes Fashion

MTV originally launched as a small-scale cable television channel in upstate New York in August 1981. It was the brainchild of a group of television **executives** who believed there was an appetite among young people for a 24-hour channel that aired nothing but music videos. They were quickly proven right. By the mid-1980s, MTV had spread throughout the entire country.

Video Hits Home

The success of MTV inspired many other television executives around the world to launch their own pop shows based on music videos. The music industry reacted to this boom by spending a lot more money on making music videos to promote their artists and their songs.

The Jackson Effect

One artist who mastered the music video format was Michael Jackson. He hired leading movie director John Landis to make an extravagant video for the song *Thriller*. The Halloween-themed clip lasted 14 minutes and cost more than $500,000 to make. It featured Jackson dancing with a troupe of zombies and was hugely successful.

Fashion Icons

Michael Jackson wasn't the only pop star setting trends in the '80s. Some teenagers wore the same ripped jeans and studded leather jackets sported by big heavy metal and rock bands such as Poison and Aerosmith. Others dressed in designer Adidas or Nike shoes and casual sportswear, just like their hip-hop idols Run–D.M.C. and The Beastie Boys.

Fad Boys and Sporty Girls

Many other fashion fads in the 1980s were inspired by music videos. The leotard-and-leggings look in Olivia Newton-John's *Physical* single, the baggy parachute pants of MC Hammer, and the frilly shirts and historical costumes worn by Adam and the Ants all set fashion trends. Thanks to these music videos, along with many others, fashion was a rapidly changing phenomenon in the '80s.

Use It Up and Wear It Out

Thanks to the music video boom of the 1980s, teenagers could see exactly what their favorite pop stars were wearing. This meant that a pop star with their own distinct look and an impressive video to match could quickly influence clothing trends. It also meant that fashions changed very quickly.

Pop music and fashion were closely linked in the 1980s. The popular "Frankie Says Relax" T-shirts were inspired by a number one song by British band Frankie Goes to Hollywood.

The Scoop

Michael Jackson's *Thriller* was one of the most **iconic** music videos of the 1980s. It was more popular than many movies, and was even shown in movie theaters. Kids across the US rushed to re-create Jackson's distinct look, which featured tight red leather pants, a red and white leather jacket, and a single white glove.

Madonna

Few pop stars have set quite as many fashion trends as Madonna. Since first storming the international pop charts in 1983, Madonna has constantly remained one step ahead of her pop rivals. In the process, she's become one of the top fashion icons of the last 30 years.

Icon in Waiting

Madonna has always been fascinated by fashion. In the late 1970s and early 1980s, she hung out at the most trendsetting New York nightclubs. When she scored a contract with Sire Records in 1982, she quickly joined forces with New York designer Maripol to create a distinctive look that would get her noticed.

From the earliest days of her career, Madonna frequently changed her look to reflect the latest cutting-edge fashion designs.

Pop Rebel

With the assistance of Maripol, Madonna created a **provocative** look that combined bold punk elements, religious icons such as **crucifixes**, and underwear worn over her clothing. She often wore lace tops, **fishnet stockings** and skirts over **capri pants**.

Clothes Horse

Madonna continued to change her style and appearance throughout the 1980s and '90s. Her world tours offered the opportunity to display outrageous new costumes. In 1990, she asked leading French fashion designer Jean Paul Gaultier to design the outfits for her *Blond Ambition* tour. He created a number of designs that went on to become fashion classics.

Design for Life

By the mid 1990s, Madonna was fully aware of her worth to fashion designers. Her videos and concerts were viewed by millions of people around the world. Many designers were eager to work with her.

Gaga Inspiration

Madonna continues to **reinvent** her look, something that contemporary stars such as Lady Gaga have copied.

Trendsetter

Even before fame, Madonna's look was unique and owed much to the New York club scene, but soon it would be the style of choice for teenage girls around the world. When she set out on her first world tour in 1985, she was amazed to see girls in the audience dressed like her. It was all due to her music videos, which were played endlessly on MTV.

Since the 1990s, Madonna has dressed as a cowgirl, worn clothing inspired by the **Kabbalah** religion, and portrayed herself as a 1970s disco **diva** in hot pants and tight tops.

TIMELINE: Madonna

1983: Scores her first international hit with *Holiday*

1985: Tours the world, showcasing costumes designed by Maripol

1990: Works with French designer Jean Paul Gaultier for the first time

1993: Features clothes designed by Dolce

& Gabbana in her *Blond Ambition* tour

1997: Dresses as a cowgirl to promote her *Ray of Light* album

2006: Features clothing from many top designers in her *Confessions* tour

2010: Designs a line of eyewear for Dolce & Gabbana

CHAPTER TWO

PEACE, LOVE, AND HATE

The relationship between music, fashion, and style goes way beyond the designer brands and **personal stylists** of top pop stars. Followers of **underground** and **alternative** music styles have always used clothes, hairstyles, and makeup to help them stand out from the crowd.

Rebel Wear

Dressing in a certain way shows others that you're a fan or follower of a certain type of music or cultural belief. This was certainly true of people who identified themselves as hippies in the late 1960s.

Hippie Roots

The hippie movement began in the US in the mid-1960s, when a writer named Ken Kesey and a group called The Merry Pranksters traveled around the country in a bus, spreading their message of peace, love, and nonconformity. By 1967, their ideas had caught on in California, specifically in a district of San Francisco known as Haight-Ashbury.

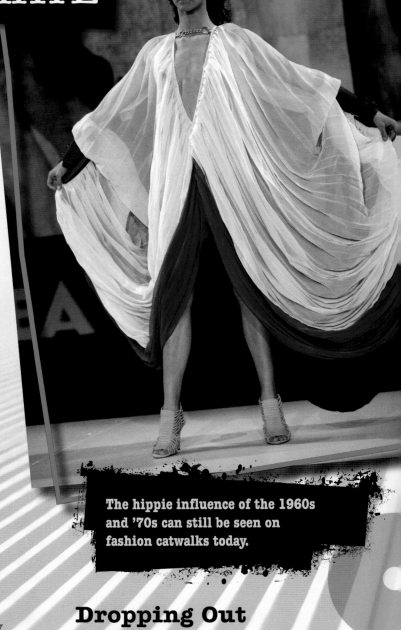

The hippie influence of the 1960s and '70s can still be seen on fashion catwalks today.

Dropping Out

At the height of the hippie movement, like-minded people from all over the US would travel to Haight-Ashbury to "turn on, tune in, and drop out." Hippies spent their time in local parks, playing and listening to music, enjoying the company of other hippies, and protesting US involvement in the **Vietnam War**.

Hippie Days

Musical, cultural, and artistic influences came together in the way hippies dressed. They wore loose shirts that featured handmade tie-dye patterns or Indian-style embroidery, headscarves, and bell-bottom pants. Men and women both grew their hair long and wore homemade jewelry.

Cultural Movement

Many famous bands, including The Beatles, The Monkees, and The Rolling Stones, began wearing "hippie" style clothing and making music inspired by the hippie culture.

Like many bands of the time, The Monkees fell in love with the hippie style of the late 1960s.

The Scoop

The hippie look of the 1960s and '70s still influences the way people dress—including pop stars, models, and actors. Since the mid 2000s, a look called "Boho chic" has been made popular by stars and stylists, such as Rachel Zoe.

The Sex Pistols

Punk rock has its roots in early-1970s New York. Young bands, such as The Ramones, did not like the excesses of mainstream rock and pop. As a reaction, they created deliberately loud and simple music— punk. By the end of the decade, punk had become more than just music for moody teenagers. It was a fashion movement, as well.

Vivienne Westwood (right) leans against a telephone booth with other punk girls on a London street in 1977.

The Story Begins

In 1975, punk rock musicians Steve Jones and Paul Cook went to a fashionable clothing shop on the King's Road in Chelsea, London, called Too Fast To Live, Too Young To Die. The shop was run by Malcolm McLaren and his designer girlfriend, Vivienne Westwood.

Making History

Jones and Cook wanted to talk to McLaren about managing their band, The Strand. The businessman had been to New York and was inspired by the outrageous looks of The Ramones and New York Dolls. Jones and Cook thought McLaren could help them hit the big time.

20

Rough Cut

McLaren and Westwood spotted an opportunity. Westwood had started designing clothes inspired by the US punk rock movement. If McLaren managed Cook and Jones' band, Westwood could style them with her new punk fashion designs. It was a great plan, and the outrageous group (renamed The Sex Pistols by McLaren) very quickly became the most famous UK band of 1976.

The Punk Look

At the time, most bands wore bold and garish clothes inspired by disco, such as jumpsuits and glittery shirts. Westwood dressed The Sex Pistols in ripped jeans, leather jackets held together by safety pins, and T-shirts featuring provocative **slogans**. They were encouraged to be as **controversial** as possible.

Fashion Movement

By the summer of 1977, punk music and fashion had become an obsession with British and US teenagers. Westwood's clothes proved

The Sex Pistols' torn clothes and rowdy live shows inspired a whole new fashion movement—punk.

the inspiration for the new punk look. Young men and women made their own punk outfits using safety pins, chains, studded leather jackets, and ripped T-shirts.

The End of the Pistols

The Sex Pistols released their debut album in 1977, but split up in 1978 at the end of their first sell-out tour in the US. By then, punk rock and fashion were firmly established in the hearts of teenagers across the world.

TIMELINE: Punk

1975: Businessman Malcolm McLaren visits New York and is excited by the new punk fashions of The New York Dolls

1976: The Sex Pistols form and are dressed by fashion designer Vivienne Westwood

1994: Green Day makes pop-punk mainstream worldwide

2000: Pop-punk continues its rise due to the success of The Offspring and Blink-182

2002: Soccer player David Beckham wears a punk-inspired **mohawk** haircut

TWO TRIBES

The early 1980s were an exciting time for underground music, with new sounds and styles appearing constantly. Each new sound had its own look, and the music videos on MTV served as a medium to publicize these fashions.

Darkness and Misery

One of the most popular underground music styles at the time was goth (short for "gothic"). This brand of **indie rock** appealed to teenagers in the US and UK due to its dark, moody sounds and suffering lyrics. Leading goth bands such as The Cult, Joy Division, and The Cure often wore dark clothing and makeup, dyeing their hair jet-black to complete the striking look.

Don't Stop the Goth

Fans of gothic rock often wore similar clothing to identify themselves with the musical movement. The typical goth look was inspired by a combination of different historical influences, such as the Victorian and Elizabethan eras. The goth look also influenced the early style of singer Madonna.

The classic gothic look evolved from a mix of horror films, dark 1980s pop music, and clothes from the 1800s.

22

Future Heads

Another popular music-inspired youth movement was "futurism." The 1980s "futurists" were fans of cutting-edge **electronic music** and **synthesizer pop**. Following bands such as Duran Duran, Depeche Mode, The Human League, and Cabaret Voltaire, young futurists wore eyeliner, long trench coats, leather pants, and baggy white shirts. Some futurists also wore blue flight jackets and lanyards (cords) instead of jewelry.

New Rock

Futurism wasn't quite as popular in the US. Many US teenagers weren't interested in music made using synthesizers, and preferred a loud new style of rock—heavy metal. Heavy metal and heavy rock bands were deliberately outrageous. They made very loud music and lived wild lifestyles. They grew their hair long, and wore ripped jeans, denim jackets, and sleeveless T-shirts or vests. Bands such as Van Halen, Kiss, Aerosmith, Iron Maiden, Judas Priest, and Def Leppard became huge stars, and it wasn't long before US teenagers were copying their style.

Get the Look

Not all US teenagers were fans of heavy rock and heavy metal. Some wore casual sportswear similar to their hip-hop idols, and others wore T-shirts with slogans. Many opted for the T-shirt/jacket combination worn by white "blue-eyed soul" acts such as Hall and Oates, while others styled their hair in the **jheri curl** style worn by funk singers such as Prince.

The Scoop

Phil Oakey did a lot to popularize the "futurist" look. He was the lead singer of a new wave synth-pop band called The Human League, and his distinctive haircut featured long bangs combed to the right. This look was copied by many of his fans.

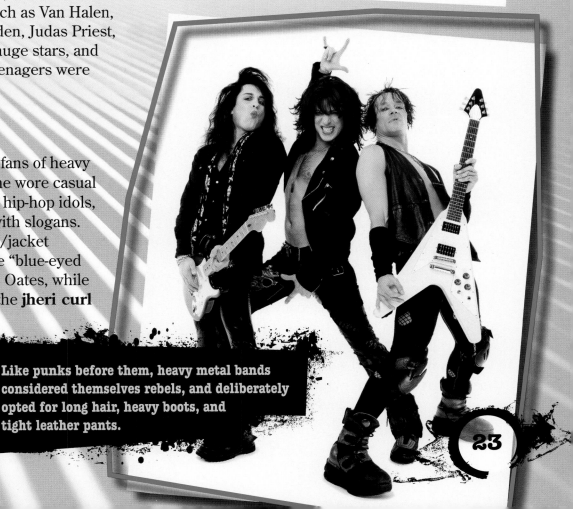

Like punks before them, heavy metal bands considered themselves rebels, and deliberately opted for long hair, heavy boots, and tight leather pants.

23

ROUGH TRADE

In the early 1990s, a form of indie-rock music called **grunge** took the world by storm. In the process, its casually dressed stars set a new fashion trend for dressing down, rather than up.

The Seattle Sound

The roots of grunge were planted in the US city of Seattle in the mid- to late 1980s. There, a number of energetic but deliberately **under-produced** rock bands recorded a whole new style of music for a small record label called Sub Pop. Groups such as Sonic Youth, Soundgarden, and Pearl Jam excited music fans with the rawness of their music, which was at odds with the glossy mainstream rock sound of the time.

Smells Like Teen Spirit

The band that helped launch grunge to a wider audience was Nirvana. Led by their **charismatic** frontman Kurt Cobain, who died tragically in 1994, Nirvana wowed listeners with their brilliant 1991 album *Nevermind*. The album contained a song that would become an anthem for a generation of music lovers—"Smells Like Teen Spirit."

Early indie rock acts, such as Sonic Youth, found their clothes in thrift stores.

Anti-fashion

Like other grunge bands of the period, Nirvana wasn't particularly bothered about fashion. On stage and in their popular music videos, they wore faded T-shirts and stained denim jeans they bought at second-hand stores. They rarely bothered combing their hair, instead leaving it unwashed and unruly. The grunge look was not so much fashionable as it was "anti-fashion."

New Trend

The casual, almost disheveled, look seen in grunge bands would go on to set a trend for indie rock music. It became fashionable to dress in old, tattered, or well-worn clothes. Soon, MTV was full of videos featuring scruffy indie rock and grunge bands. Mainstream fashion designers began to take note.

Fashion Fix

The fashion industry responded to the grunge movement by creating new clothes with a grunge look. They also used some of the scene's biggest stars to sell their wares.

Geek Chic

British indie rock bands quickly followed the trend set by their US peers. Early-1990s "**shoegazing**" bands wore baggy, long-sleeved T-shirts along with jeans and Dr. Martens boots. Later, 1990s bands, such as Pulp, dressed primarily in geek chic outfits featuring faded 1970s clothing rescued from thrift stores.

Lasting Legacy

The casual grunge look set a trend in indie rock music that still exists to this day. Since grunge hit the mainstream, most indie rock bands and fans dress casually in jeans, T-shirts, and battered tennis shoes or Dr. Martens boots.

The Scoop

When asked during a magazine interview to explain the popularity of the grunge look, Sub Pop Records boss Jonathan Poneman said: "The clothing is cheap, durable, and **timeless**. It also runs against the grain of the whole flashy **aesthetic** that existed in the 1980s."

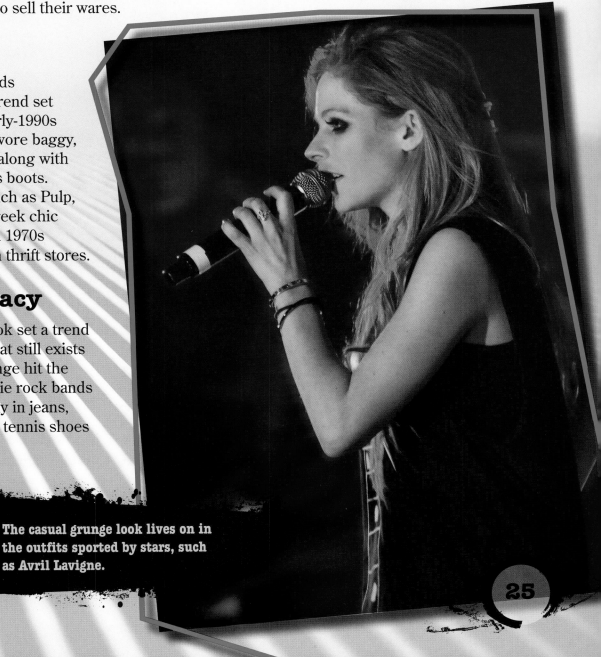

The casual grunge look lives on in the outfits sported by stars, such as Avril Lavigne.

CHAPTER THREE

BEAT THE STREET

The hip-hop revolution brought its own sense of style—not to mention a love of designer sportswear, shoes, and sports caps.

One of the biggest shifts in fashion over the last three decades has been the growth of streetwear. This is fashion inspired by the casual, but often stylish, day-to-day outfits of young people. The origins of these outfits can often be traced back to recording artists and their videos or their specific music scene. This is certainly the case with the original streetwear **phenomenon**—hip-hop.

Get Sporty

Back in the early 1980s when rap music and hip-hop culture were first surfacing, the idea of wearing sportswear as a fashion choice was exciting. Before this, the only people who wore sportswear were athletes.

Ruthless Rap Assassins

In the mid-1980s, the world was beginning to wake up to a form of music that had emerged from the tough streets of New York City in the late 1970s. Hip-hop was performed by "rappers" who wore tracksuits, baseball caps, and chunky gold jewelry. It was like nothing that had come before.

Casual Appeal

To 1980s teenagers, especially those outside of New York, part of the appeal of hip-hop and rap music was the exciting look of the scene's new stars. To kids who'd grown up watching pop stars in designer outfits or outrageous clothes, the casual yet bold look of rappers was an amazing development. It wasn't long before hip-hop fans began to copy the clothes worn by Run–D.M.C., Kurtis Blow, and The Beastie Boys.

Hip-Hop Style

The 1980s hip-hop look was striking on one hand, and impressively casual on the other. Typical outfits would begin with basic tracksuits or T-shirts paired with baggy jeans, but would also feature gold chains, bomber jackets, and expensive shoes.

The Scoop

The 1980s rap heavyweights Run– D.M.C. summed up hip-hop's obsession with fashionable sneakers on their 1986 single "My Adidas." The track helped secure them a $1.6 million **endorsement deal** with the German sportswear giant—the first in the history of hip-hop.

The Kicks

Throughout the 1980s, the most important items in any hip-hop fan's wardrobe were their sneakers. Some fans have taken their love of sneakers to another level. These collectors refer to themselves as "sneaker heads."

Bling Beginnings

As hip-hop changed and became more popular in the 1990s and 2000s, so did the way its biggest stars dressed. It became more about wearing the hottest high-end brands, from Tommy Hilfiger to Versace and Rolex.

Marketing Magic

Major sportswear manufacturers soon realized the **potential** in marketing their clothes and athletic shoes to the hip-hop community. It was a smart move. As the popularity of hip-hop spread around the world, so did the popularity of their **premium** sportswear.

In recent years, hip-hop style has been revolutionized by the concept of "bling"— expensive jewelry featuring gold, silver, and diamonds.

THIS IS ACID

The boost in streetwear sales in the 1980s and '90s had an influence on more than just the day-to-day clothing of young people. It also changed the way people dressed to go out, just as a huge explosion in the popularity of dance music took hold on both sides of the Atlantic.

Tried and Tested

Traditionally, going to dance clubs was the highlight of many people's weekend. Men and women danced to the latest pop, soul, funk, and disco tunes in mainstream clubs.

Going Underground

Even at underground nightclubs, where young people would dance to alternative music styles, a focus on fashion was encouraged. In some cases, this would mean dressing in the style of a specific music genre—futurism, goth, or new romantic.

This Is Acid

The arrival of a new form of music called acid house changed everything. In 1988, the UK and the US experienced what became the second "summer of love." Hundreds of thousands of teenagers gathered in fields at **illegal raves** to move to the latest acid house music to hit the dance scene.

The early-1990s rave scene was founded on the principle of "being yourself." This meant that dancers should wear whatever they liked, so long as they felt comfortable.

Love and Happiness

Acid house had a profound effect on young people. Before this genre, music fans were often very **tribal** and stuck to clubs that played music they knew and liked. Acid house brought fans of many different music styles together. They just wanted to dance and have a good time.

Boom Times

On the back of the second summer of love, rock musicians began incorporating elements of dance music into their songs. Attitudes toward fashion changed.

One Love

Acid house broke down barriers in the way people dressed when they went out. Instead of wearing the tribal uniforms that identified them as fans of a certain style, teenagers began wearing more ordinary, casual clothes that were comfortable to dance in.

The Scoop

The single-most popular item among ravers in the late 1980s was the acid house smiley T-shirt, designed to portray acid house as the "simplest and gentlest" music of its time. The logo became popular after it was used in the video for Bomb the Bass's top ten single "Beat Dis."

Be Yourself

Club fashion has changed since the 1980s, but the commitment to dress comfortably and "be yourself" has remained. If you visited an underground nightclub today, you would find some people dressed in the latest fashions, some more casually, and still others in urban designs influenced by hip-hop.

Smiley culture

Athletic shoes, baggy jeans, and long-sleeved T-shirts became popular with ravers. Some revisited the loose, late-1960s look of US hippies, while others found influence in contemporary fashion, following magazines such as *Elle*.

TUNING IN

For many years, major chain stores have followed youth music trends. This has never been more apparent than in recent years. Street-savvy teenagers and young people tune in to music that takes the best of the past and present, and offers something new and fresh.

Indie-Dance Returns

There has traditionally been little **crossover** between indie rock and dance, both musically and in fashion. Yet in the mid 2000s, a new wave of indie-dance bands began to emerge. These new groups took the best of both styles and created something completely new.

Nu-rave Wave

Fashion quickly followed suit, responding to these new sounds with a distinctive look that was coined **nu-rave**. It paired the tight-fitting, low-slung skinny jeans seen on indie rockers with the off-the-shoulder women's tops and baggy T-shirts once worn by 1980s ravers.

For a brief period, nu-rave was massive. Teenagers bought music downloads by bands such as the Klaxons and Simian Mobile Disco, and dressed in typical nu-rave outfits.

Dance act Simian Mobile Disco was at the forefront of a new movement in music and fashion called nu-rave.

The Scoop

The most influential nu-rave scene in the world was based in Paris, and was centered on a record label called Ed Banger. The label's artists created their own look, using traditional rock items such as leather pants and jackets with vintage T-shirts, white-rimmed sunglasses, and 1980s-inspired haircuts.

Making a Comeback

On the back of nu-rave, many bands gained inspiration from the synthesizer sounds of the 1980s. Fashion stores once again followed suit, offering young people the chance to buy designs influenced by major 1980s clothing trends. Leggings, Lycra "pop tops," and capri pants all made a comeback, alongside clothes in bright **neon** colors.

Vintage Revival

This desire to look back for inspiration, both musically and in the way people dress, continues to this day. Vintage clothing has become increasingly popular, from 1940s- and '50s-inspired dresses, shirts, and blouses to tight-fitting T-shirts featuring designs from the 1970s and '80s.

All Change

Thanks to online access, both musical and fashion trends are constantly changing. By the time you read this, a new musical movement will have emerged, and the way young people dress will have shifted to reflect it.

The distinctive nu-rave look was inspired by a mix of early 1990s rave clothing, 80s style, and hip-hop sportswear.

Urban Warriors

Recent urban fashion items include big earrings inspired by African culture, baseball caps, and Burberry-check caps. T-shirts featuring 1980s-style slogans or hand-drawn illustrations, shorts, and both baggy and skinny jeans have also made a comeback.

BIG IN JAPAN

It's easy to think of the United States as the driving force behind pop fashion. Yet over the last two decades, one nation has embraced streetwear more than any other—Japan.

Changing Times

Traditionally, the Japanese have been quite **conservative** in the way they dress and act. Yet, as the country flourished and became more financially successful over the last 50 years, attitudes have completely changed.

Money to Burn

Young people in Japan have more money to spend than their counterparts in Europe and the US. Because of this, more CDs and music downloads are sold in Japan than in any other country except the United States. Streetwear inspired by Western pop fashion is hugely popular with the nation's young people.

Individual Style

Japanese teenagers like to dress to impress. Instead of sticking to one style, many young people create their own outfits by mixing clothing and hairstyles made popular by Western and Japanese (J-pop) musicians.

Cutting-Edge

The outfits created by young people in Japan are often far bolder and more outrageous than those worn by teenagers in the US. Department stores in Japan sell clothing many in the West would consider to be cutting-edge.

Fashion Fusion

One famous example of Japanese street fashion at its most outrageous and distinct is the Lolita look. Originally inspired by the dresses,

The Scoop

The Harajuku district of Tokyo is widely considered to be the streetwear capital of the world. It features many small fashion **boutiques** selling cutting-edge clothing designs. Every Sunday, teenagers gather in Harajuku in their best outfits to hang out with their friends.

Worldwide Success

Japanese fashion is now incredibly popular worldwide. In a neat twist, many top US rap stars now wear clothing made in Japan, such as Evisu jeans. The brand has been mentioned in tracks by Jay-Z, Young Jeezy, and Lil Wayne. The Neptunes producer Pharrell Williams is such a fan of Japanese clothing that he invested in A Bathing Ape, one of Japan's leading brands. Even singer Gwen Stefani launched her own Japanese-inspired clothing line, Harajuku Lovers, in 2005.

The popular Japanese Lolita punk style has an edgy but cute look.

corsets, and suits worn by Europeans in the nineteenth century, it has taken on many influences from 20th century musical styles. Examples of Lolita fashion include gothic, classic, and punk.

Rap Attack

Hip-hop is particularly big in Japan. Since first making an impression on Tokyo's teenagers in the early 1990s, it has shaped the way many young Japanese dress. Some Japanese hip-hop fans go even further than dressing like their rap idols, darkening their faces with makeup to look more like black Americans.

After visiting Tokyo while on tour, Gwen Stefani launched her own line of clothes inspired by Japanese style and culture.

WEB STYLE

Over the last 15 years, the Internet has changed the way people communicate, shop, and spend their leisure time. It has also had an incredible effect on the music and fashion industries.

The Dark Ages

Before the Internet, music fans got their information about new bands or upcoming releases from television, radio, newspapers, and magazines. Consequently, music and fashion trends changed relatively slowly, usually following recommendations from a handful of journalists around the world.

Everything Changes

The explosion of music and fashion blogs in the late 2000s changed everything. **Amateurs** and would-be journalists began sharing their thoughts with the world. In music, bloggers **championed** new music styles and unheard bands, while the fashion world was turned upside down by bloggers promoting little-known designers or their own ideas on bold new outfits.

Get With the Band

Many musicians and bands have capitalized on this music and fashion revolution by selling their own merchandise directly to fans online. Others collaborate with their favorite designers to launch limited edition items that are only available at concerts. More than ever, music fashion is in the hands of musicians and fans rather than traditional designers.

When stars such as Katy Perry post a photograph of themselves wearing a different hair color, it can start a new trend overnight.

She's in Fashion

In the early days, many fashion blogs were focused on high-end fashion and famous brands. One of the first fashion bloggers to find success was Kathryn Finney of *The Budget Fashionista*. Her blog was so influential, she was invited to attend New York Fashion Week in 2003.

People Power

In recent years, there has been a huge increase in blogs focusing on street fashion—fashion trends that emerge from underground music scenes, developed by real people rather than fashion designers.

Changing the Fashion World

Music and fashion blogs are particularly important to their respective industries because they influence major trends. Blogs can be updated quickly, helping fashion-conscious teenagers find the latest looks or sounds faster than ever before.

Internet fashion bloggers have replaced fashion journalists as the taste-makers of the 21st century.

The Scoop

In 2007, journalist Robin Givhan used an article in fashion magazine *Harper's Bazaar* to claim that blogs had changed the fashion business. He said, "The average person, too often **estranged** from fashion, is taking ownership of it."

Blog On

In recent years, the effect of fashion and music blogs on both industries has been vast. For example, many young, unknown T-shirt designers have created popular designs based on music icons, trends, or slogans. These sell in large amounts thanks to blog postings. The '80s revival (in music and fashion) and the rise in urban dance culture also have support from bloggers to thank for their popularity.

CHAPTER FOUR

BIG BUSINESS

In the 21st century, the lines between music, fashion, style, and business have become increasingly blurred. Many top recording artists now sign multimillion-dollar deals with clothing or cosmetics brands, while others set up their very own fashion companies.

Brand Ambassadors

Clothing brands and manufacturers of high-end fashion accessories, such as perfumes, have seen the potential of music stars acting as "brand ambassadors." Hiring a star can be a quick, if expensive, way to obtain high-profile publicity and increase awareness of a product. In most cases, the endorsement of an A-list celebrity can boost sales significantly.

Wealth Talks

In the late 20th and early 21st century, no one area of music has been more heavily involved in brand endorsements than hip-hop and R&B. In the 1990s, the scene's top stars, such as Jay-Z and Sean Paul, used their records to rap about money and wealth. "Bling bling" became a reference to expensive jewelry and flashy accessories. Top stars would regularly

Missy Elliot has a multimillion-dollar endorsement deal with German sportswear giant Adidas, and has even designed clothing for the company.

wear expensive watches and oversized jewelry. They would also rap about other products associated with great wealth, such as champagne and the world's fastest cars.

Endorsements

Given their status as huge global stars, it wasn't long before big companies began approaching musicians to endorse their products. Missy Elliot signed a contract to design and promote her own clothing line with sportswear brand Adidas, while Beyoncé launched her own brand of perfume, True Star, with Tommy Hilfiger.

The Scoop

One R&B artist who has profited substantially from product endorsements is Rihanna. In the last decade, she has had endorsement deals with cosmetics brands Nivea and Clinique, sportswear brand Nike, and top **fashion house** Gucci.

Fashion Future

Some global hip-hop stars are not happy endorsing other people's products and have moved into fashion themselves. A number of top rappers now own huge clothing and fashion companies, and they use their star status to promote their labels.

Fashion Billionaires

Many big hip-hop stars now have business interests in the fashion world. The Neptunes producer Pharrell Williams owns a clothing company called Billionaire Boys Club, which he founded with Japanese fashion designer Nigo. Until 2007, Jay-Z was also part-owner of urban fashion brand Rocawear. Beyoncé owns a clothing company called House of Dereon, and 50 Cent has a multimillion-dollar deal with Reebok.

P. Diddy

One of the most successful rappers-turned-businessmen is Sean Combs. He launched his line of fashionable men's clothing, Sean John, in 1998. Since then, it has grown to be one of the most popular lines in the US, winning fashion design awards. In 2008, he added to his fashion interests by purchasing the Enyce clothing brand.

Grace Jones

Many musicians embrace the opportunity to be outfitted by top fashion designers. The relationship between underground music and high-end fashion goes back a long way, and since the 1970s, no one has paired these two cultures quite like Grace Jones.

Striking Model

Born in the Caribbean, Grace Jones first made a name for herself as a runway model in New York, Paris, London, and Milan in the mid-1970s. As a tall black woman with striking looks and haircuts usually worn by men, she was one of the most distinctive and in-demand models of her time.

Having started her career as a runway model for top fashion designers, singer Grace Jones knows more than most pop stars about cutting-edge and outrageous costumes.

38

Pop Art

While in New York, Jones befriended famous artist Andy Warhol, who led the pop art movement of the 1950s and '60s. He photographed the model and took her to Studio 54, the most famous club of the era.

New York Icon

Because of her looks, famous modeling career, and love of disco music, Jones quickly became an icon in New York's gay scene. And it wasn't long before Island Records offered her a recording contract.

Grace's Portfolio

Jones released her first album, a collection of disco tracks called *Portfolio*, in 1977. Although it wasn't a huge success, Jones recorded two more disco albums before switching her attention to reggae and new wave pop. Because of Jones' modeling career, her records received plenty of press coverage.

Rhythm Queen

In 1985, Jones released her most widely acclaimed project, a concept album entitled *Slave to the Rhythm*. Unlike regular albums, it didn't feature a set of songs, but rather various interpretations of the title track. It was

Bond Girl

Grace Jones' most famous film role was as unlikely Bond girl May Day in the 1985 James Bond movie *A View to a Kill*. She starred alongside Roger Moore and the film's villain, Christopher Walken.

adventurous and lived up to her reputation as a force at the forefront of fashion and music.

She's a Model

Slave to the Rhythm contained a number of references to Jones' modeling career. One of the tracks was called "The Fashion Show," while others featured interviews with the singer.

Groundbreaking

Slave to the Rhythm was one of the most significant records of the 1980s. It perfectly summed up the working relationship between underground club culture, cutting-edge electronic music, and high fashion.

TIMELINE: Grace Jones

1975: Begins modeling career, sharing a Paris apartment with Jerry Hall

1977: Lands record deal with Island Records

1981: Releases *Pullup to the Bumper*, her biggest club hit

1985: Stars as May Day in the James Bond movie *A View to a Kill*

2006: Walks the catwalk at the age of 57 for Diesel's New York show

2008: Named Q Idol at the *Q Magazine* Awards for her services to music and fashion

THE BRIT SCENE

In the 1960s, a rise in popularity of British music around the world, and particularly in the US, led to a renewed focus on the country's fashion scene. Britain's fashion, style, and cosmetics industries received a similar boost in the 1990s and early 2000s thanks to a new boom in British music.

Dual Inspirations

There were two inspirations for this British revival. First, there was Britpop, a form of indie rock music that borrowed heavily from the sounds of 1960s swinging London. Then, there were The Spice Girls, a pop band aimed at teenage girls, who became superstars around the world.

God Save the Queen

Both The Spice Girls and Britpop heroes, such as Oasis and Blur, were proud of their British roots. Oasis songwriter Noel Gallagher often appeared on stage with a guitar featuring the country's Union Jack flag, while Blur's songs focused on life in London.

Spice World

The Spice Girls showed their support for British culture by wearing such clothing as Union Jack dresses.

When Spice Girls singer Geri Halliwell appeared at the Brit Awards wearing a Union Jack dress, it launched a whole new craze for British fashion designs.

They starred in their own movie, *Spice World*, which featured a London double-decker bus painted in Britain's colors.

Cool Britannia

The Spice Girls and Oasis had great success in the US. Their brands of British pop were a hit with teenagers and 20-something music buyers. It wasn't long before magazines such

as *Rolling Stone* and *Newsweek* were writing that London was "swinging" again. The British revival was dubbed "Cool Britannia"—a pun on the **patriotic** British song "Rule Britannia."

The Scoop

The term "Cool Britannia" was first used in the 1960s, but became popular in the 1990s, thanks to ice cream makers Ben & Jerry's. They **trademarked** the term when they named a limited-edition flavor of ice cream containing British staples such as strawberries, cream, and shortbread cookie pieces.

Fashion Boom

Cool Britannia was about more than music. With London once again the center of attention, the British fashion industry enjoyed a new period of global dominance. British models Kate Moss and Naomi Campbell became the poster girls for clothing by British fashion designers Alexander McQueen and Stella McCartney.

Swinging London Town

In 1997, leading fashion magazine *Vanity Fair* published a special issue under the headline "London Swings Again." It featured Oasis singer Liam Gallagher and actress Patsy Kensit on the cover, plus interviews with Alexander McQueen and Blur guitarist Graham Coxon.

The face of London

Model Kate Moss was one of the key figures in Cool Britannia. She not only modeled the latest British fashions, but also hung out with top pop stars in London. She quickly became the face of the Rimmel makeup brand, which relaunched as Rimmel London to cash in on the US passion for British products.

Model Kate Moss was a central figure in what the press called "Cool Britannia"— an upsurge in the popularity of British clothing and music in the late 1990s.

41

Lady Gaga

Madonna built a long career as an entertainer by wearing outrageous costumes and by having close relationships with top fashion designers. Today, there is a new queen of pop fashion— Lady Gaga.

Global Icon

Lady Gaga has sold millions of CDs worldwide. Her single *Poker Face* is reportedly one of the most downloaded songs of all time. Yet just as Madonna before her, Lady Gaga has built her reputation on more than just music. First entering the pop charts in 2007, she is known just as much for her cutting-edge style as for her catchy songs.

Dressed for Success

During her time as a **burlesque** performer, Lady Gaga began to play around with her on-stage look. She created outfits that mixed the glam rock style of David Bowie, disco

Lady Gaga is as famous for her outrageous clothing as she is for her top-selling pop hits.

glamour, Madonna's revolutionary early 1980s look, and contemporary catwalk fashions.

Over the Top

Lady Gaga didn't stop with mainstream fads of the past. She added influences from the burlesque scene, such as intense makeup and over-the-top hairstyles. By the time she became a global star in the late 2000s, she'd created a daring and outrageous look all her own.

Talking Point

Since making it big, Lady Gaga has received just as much coverage in the fashion world as she has in the realm of music. For every new live show, she introduces a string of new outfits. She works with a variety of both well-known and up-and-coming fashion designers in order to stay ahead of her rivals.

Award Winner

In 2010, Lady Gaga was listed as one of *British Vogue*'s "10 Best Dressed People" of the year, while her stylist Nicola Formichetti was named Fashion Creator of the Year at the 2010 British Fashion Awards. Lady Gaga also writes a column for US fashion magazine *V*, regarding the designs of her unique outfits.

Underground Beginnings

Before she became a big star, Lady Gaga —born Stefani Germanotta—spent time in various underground bands, playing electronic and alternative rock music. Unable to secure a record contract, she instead began singing and dancing in underground New York clubs, specifically, the controversial burlesque scene.

Lasting Influence

Although operating at the more cutting-edge end of fashion, Lady Gaga has also had a huge effect on high street fashion in Europe and the US. Her passion for outrageous outfits has caught on with mainstream designers and her young audience. In just the short time in which she has risen to fame, she has become an iconic figure in pop fashion.

TIMELINE: Lady Gaga

2005: Records her first professional song with rap legend Grandmaster Melle Mel

2006: Adopts Lady Gaga name and works as a burlesque performer

2007: Signs to Interscope Records

2008: Debut single *Just Dance* rockets to the top of the US charts

2010: Causes controversy by wearing a dress made from meat

2011: Releases her biggest-selling album yet, *Born This Way*

GLOSSARY

aesthetic how something looks

alternative different

amateurs enthusiastic people who do something as an unpaid hobby

blueprint a detailed plan

boutiques small, independently run shops

burlesque a style of entertainment featuring songs, dancing, and comedy routines that became popular in the 19th century

capri pants a style of mid-calf pants, often worn by women

championing campaigning for or enthusiastically talking about something

charismatic someone who is persuasive and charming

conservative to be traditional or cautious of change

controversial something that causes debate between people

creative expression anything that allows someone to be creative, for example, designing clothes or making music

crossover the point where two or more music or fashion styles come together to form something new

crucifixes the Christian symbol of a cross

diva a celebrated female singer

double-breasted a coat or suit jacket featuring two parallel rows of buttons and overlapping flaps

drainpipe trousers pants with very skinny legs

electronic music music made using computers and electronic instruments, such as keyboards and drum machines

endorsement deal an agreement in which a star wears a company's clothing or shoes in exchange for payment

establishment a term used to refer to people in positions of power, for example, politicians, policemen, and business people

estranged separated

executives the head people of a big company, such as a record label

fashion house a fashion industry term for a company that makes fashionable clothing

fishnet stockings stockings featuring a diamond stitch pattern

grunge a popular style of 1990s US rock music, so-called because of the casual, often unwashed clothes worn by bands

iconic famous and memorable

identity what makes people distinguishable, such as their clothes, personality, or taste in music

illegal raves big, unlicensed dance music events, often held outdoors

indie rock alternative rock music–"indie" is short for "independent"

influential someone or something that helps to change the way people think or act

jheri curl a 1980s hairstyle featuring tight curls, popular among black musicians

Kabbalah a traditional religion based on Judaism (a Jewish religion)

kilt a traditional Scottish item of clothing for men and women that resembles a skirt

mainstream popular and well-known

mop-top a popular 1960s haircut inspired by The Beatles

neon very bright colors that don't look natural

nu-rave a mid-2000s music and fashion movement inspired by clothes, makeup, and dance music of the early 1990s

patriotic to be proud of your nationality

personal stylists people who assist stars with their makeup and clothing choices

phenomenon a massive or unusual event

pioneers people who do something first before anyone else

44

polyester a man-made fabric

pop culture a collective term for music, art, books, fashion, films, and television

potential capable of becoming something, for example, an up-and-coming musician

premium expensive or top of the line

promote to encourage the sale of something by publicizing it, for example through advertisements or media interviews

provocative designed to get an extreme reaction from viewers or listeners

R&B a popular style of soul music–short for "rhythm and blues"

reinvent to come up with a whole new style, sound, or personality from scratch

revival to bring something back, for example, old music or clothing trends

rivalry heated competition between two or more people, or groups of people

shoegazing a style of British rock music popular in the early 1990s, so-called because of their despondent approach when performing

slogans phrases or mottos used to sell products

synthesizer pop a style of popular music largely made using synthesizer keyboards

tailors people who make clothes for a living

timeless something that lasts the test of time, such as a style of clothing or piece of music

trademarked something protected by a "trademark" (a binding legal document)

tribal to share common characteristics within a community, for example, those who share a taste in music or clothing

under-produced music designed to sound raw, unpolished, or unfinished

underground alternative or less popular

Vietnam War a war in Vietnam, Asia, between 1955 and 1975, in which 58,000 US soldiers and over 2 million Vietnamese died

Books

Cally Blackman. *100 Years of Fashion Illustration* (Laurence King Publishers, 2007).

Bonnie English. *Fashion: The 50 Most Influential Fashion Designers of All Time* (Barron's Educational Series, 2010).

Bonnie English. *A Cultural History of Fashion in the 20th Century: From the Catwalk to the Sidewalk* (Berg Publishers, 2007).

The Teen Vogue Handbook: An Insider's Guide to Careers in Fashion (Puffin, 2010).

Websites

Find out more about streetwear from around the world at:
www.streetpeeper.com

Visit this international magazine's website to discover more about music and fashion:
www.musicfashionmagazine.com

Read the online edition of leading British fashion and music magazine *Dazed & Confused* at:
www.dazeddigital.com

INDEX

50 Cent 7, 37

acid house 28, 29
Adam and the Ants 15
Aerosmith 15, 23

Bay City Rollers, The 13
Beach Boys, The 10
Beastie Boys, The 15, 26
Beatles, The 10, 11, 19
Beyoncé 36, 37
Blink-182 21
Blow, Kurtis 26
Blur 40, 41
Boho chic 19
Bomb the Bass 29
Bowie, David 12, 43
Britpop 40

Cabaret Voltaire 23
clothing companies 7, 15,
    17, 27, 31, 36, 37
clothing stores 7, 10, 30,
    32, 43
Combs, Sean 7, 37
concert tours 6, 17, 21, 33,
    34
Cook, Paul 20, 21
Cooper, Alice 12
Cult, The 22
Cure, The 22

dance music 6, 8, 12, 13, 14,
    28, 29, 30, 35
Dean, James 8
Def Leppard 23
Depeche Mode 23
designers 7, 12, 13, 16, 17,
    20, 21, 25, 34, 35, 37, 38,
    41, 42, 43
disco 12, 13, 17, 21, 28, 39,
    43
Duran Duran 23

electronic music 23, 39,
    43, 44
endorsement deal 27, 36,
    37, 44
Epstein, Brian 10

fans 6, 7, 9, 10, 12, 13, 18,
    22, 23, 24, 25, 26, 27, 29,
    33, 34
Frankie Goes to Hollywood
    15
futurism 23, 28

Gaultier, Jean Paul 17
Geek chic 25
goth 6, 9, 22, 28, 33
Green Day 21
grunge 6, 24, 25, 44

hairstyles 6, 7, 8, 9, 10, 11,
    18, 19, 21, 22, 23, 24, 30,
    32, 34, 38, 43
Hall and Oates 23
heavy metal 6, 15, 23
hip-hop 6, 7, 9, 15, 23, 26,
    27, 29, 31, 33, 36, 37
hippies 18, 19, 29
Holly, Buddy 8
Human League, The 23

Iggy Pop 12
indie rock 22, 24, 25, 30,
    40, 44
Internet 31, 34, 35
Iron Maiden 23

Jackson, Michael 14, 15
Japan 32, 33, 37
Jay-Z 7, 33, 36, 37
jewelry 17, 19, 21, 23, 26,
    27, 31, 36
Jones, Grace 38, 39
Jones, Steve 20, 21
Joy Division 22
Judas Priest 23

Kiss 23
Klaxons 30

Lady Gaga 17, 42, 43
Landis, John 14
Lavigne, Avril 25
Lil Wayne 33
Lolita look 32, 33
London 10, 11, 12, 20, 38,
    40, 41

Madonna 16, 17, 22, 42, 43
makeup 6, 7, 12, 13, 18, 22,
    33, 36, 37, 40. 41, 42, 43
MC Hammer 15
McLaren, Malcolm 20, 21
media 14, 25, 29, 34, 35, 39,
    40, 41, 43
Missy Elliot 36
models 19, 38, 39, 41
Monkees, The 19
Moss, Kate 41
movies 8, 11, 13, 14, 15, 22,
    39, 40
MTV 14, 17, 22, 25

New York 13, 14, 16, 17, 20,
    21, 26, 35, 38, 39, 43
New York Dolls 20
Newton-John, Olivia 15
Nirvana 24
nu-rave 30, 31, 44

Oakey, Phil 23
Oasis 40, 41
Offspring, The 21

Paul, Sean 36
Pearl Jam 24
perfume 7, 36
Perry, Katy 34
Poison 15
Presley, Elvis 8
Prince 23
promotion 10, 14, 17, 27,
    36, 37, 45
Pulp 25
punk 6, 17, 20, 21, 23, 33

Quant, Mary 12

R&B 36, 37, 45
Ramones, The 20, 21
rave 6, 9, 28, 29, 30, 31, 44
record companies 16, 24,
    25, 30, 39
Reed, Lou 12
reggae 39
religious influences 17
revival 11, 31, 35, 40, 41, 45
Rihanna 37
rock 12, 15, 20, 21, 22, 23,
    24, 25, 29, 30, 40, 43
rock and roll 8, 9, 10, 11
Rolling Stones, The 19
Run–D.M.C. 15, 26, 27

Sex Pistols, The 20, 21
shoegazing bands 25, 45
Simian Mobile Disco 30
slogans 21, 23, 31, 34, 45
Sonic Youth 24
Soundgarden 24
Spears, Britney 7
Spice Girls, The 40
sportswear 6, 15, 23, 26, 27,
    31, 36, 37
Stefani, Gwen 33
streetwear 26, 28, 32, 35
stylists 7, 18, 19, 43, 45
sunglasses 17, 30
synthesizer pop 23, 31, 45

Teddy Boys 9
Travolta, John 13
T. Rex 12

underground 18, 22, 28, 29,
    35, 38, 39, 43, 45
underwear 5, 17, 23, 33

Van Halen 23
videos 7, 14, 15, 17, 22, 24,
    25, 26, 29
Vincent, Gene 8
vintage clothing 11, 30, 31

Warhol, Andy 39
Westwood, Vivienne 20, 21
Who, The 11
Williams, Pharrell 33, 37
Winehouse, Amy 11

Young Jeezy 33